D E M O C R A T I C

N A T I O N A L

C O N V E N T I O N

2 0 0 8

O B A M A's

Mile High

M O M E N T

DEMOCRATIC NATIONAL CONVENTION 2008

OBAMA's *Mile High* MOMENT

THE DENVER POST

FULCRUM
GOLDEN, COLORADO

In 2005, THE SAME YEAR BARACK OBAMA RAISED HIS hand to be sworn in as a US senator, Denver's Elbra Wedgeworth raised hers and asked the Democratic Party why its national convention shouldn't travel west to the Rockies. Their aspirations made a political match to last through 2008 and beyond, propelling a city, a party, and a nation.

People said Denver wasn't big enough to hold a modern Democratic National Convention. America, they said, wasn't big enough to nominate a junior senator from Illinois as the first African American presidential nominee in major party history.

"They" were wrong. The 2008 Democratic National Convention brought a proud candidate to a proud city in order to form a most perfect union. The people painted their faces over it, cried over it, went to jail for it, and even quit their jobs to come see it. A mile high and an epoch wide, the convention was bigger than the words used to describe it.

For three years after then Denver city council president Wedgeworth raised her hand, civic leaders endured a whirlwind of posturing, desperate fund-raising, meticulous planning, and ominous threats. Could the city handle the Democrats? Could the Democrats handle Obama?

Over thirty-six months, Denver and Obama grew so confident in their obliteration of tradition that they ended up inviting 84,000 people to celebrate their victory together.

Everybody came. No one wanted to miss something this big. Not the historians seeking to document the first black presidential candidate nominated by a major

Democratic presidential hopeful senator Barack Obama, opposite page, *waves to the crowd inside the Pepsi Center a day before accepting his party's nomination.*

"THIS MOMENT —THIS ELECTION— IS OUR CHANCE TO KEEP, IN THE TWENTY-FIRST CENTURY, THE AMERICAN PROMISE ALIVE."

—Democratic presidential nominee Senator Barack Obama

party. Not the Democrats dreaming of an end to Republican rule. Not the citizens of Denver longing for national recognition. And not the Coloradans simply enjoying another perfect August evening under the stars at their football stadium.

The 2008 Democratic National Convention preoccupied a city from August 25 to August 28, and every day told a story.

There were the protests that threatened chaos and destruction, ending in photo opportunities with smiling anarchists and chagrined SWAT teams. The week's casualties: only 154 arrests and a few shots of pepper spray, making the special detention warehouse obsolete before it opened.

There was aging Teddy of the mythological Kennedy clan, piling fairy tale upon legend by rising from his sickbed and rousing the delegates from his Pepsi Center podium. "This November, the torch will be passed again to a new generation of Americans," shouted Kennedy, who was recovering from brain cancer surgery. "The work begins anew. The hope rises again. And the dream lives on."

"THIS NOVEMBER, THE TORCH WILL BE PASSED AGAIN TO A NEW GENERATION OF AMERICANS. THE WORK BEGINS ANEW. THE HOPE RISES AGAIN. AND THE DREAM LIVES ON."

—*Senator Ted Kennedy*

There was working mom Michelle Obama pulling off the difficult trick of appearing dazzling and down-to-earth in the same speech. "I come here as a mom whose girls are the heart of my heart and the center of my world," the candidate's wife said. "They're the first thing I think about when I wake up in the morning and the last thing I think about when I go to bed at night. Their future and all our children's future is my stake in this election."

There was celebrity-spotting without even trying, as stars from Charlize Theron and Jessica Alba to Sean Penn and Spike Lee wandered Denver without the usual excuse of a film festival.

There were angry Hillary Rodham Clinton delegates finally letting go, in the face of Obama-mania and a universally lauded grace note from their pant-suited leader on Tuesday night. An ultimate fighting match for the soul of the party never materialized as Hillary took to a floor microphone Wednesday to nominate Obama by acclamation.

"Let's declare together, right here, right now, that Barack Obama is our candidate and he will be our next president," Clinton said, touching off a rowdy floor dance accompanied by "Love Train" on the PA system.

There was Denver mayor John Hickenlooper blinking in the bright lights of the stage his dogged fund-raising helped build. Fresh from completing his $40 million fund-raising marathon, Hickenlooper finally got to tell his own story of rising up, from laid-off geologist to beer-house baron to the city's top pol.

"Change has served me well," Hickenlooper said. "It has served Denver well over its 150-year history. And change is the only thing that can restart our nation's economy and realign our nation's compass."

There were countless ordinary sojourners, such as twenty-four-year-old delegate Jacob Krapl of Iowa, wearing his Iraq combat boots into the convention hall to remind partying Democrats of a war they oppose.

There was Bill Clinton, loose and generous and beloved, when pundits had worried he'd be the opposite of all three.

There was Senator Joe Biden, solid if a bit uninspiring, happy to be invited to the show.

And then there was Invesco Field at Mile High, surrounded by mazes of security fencing and Secret Service barriers, buzzing with helicopters and cut off by the impenetrable moat of an unprecedented Interstate 25 shutdown. Denver bristled with more than 2,000 peace officers, and all the handcuffs and shields that $50 million in federal security aid could buy.

Longtime volunteers and recent Obama enthusiasts vied for the "golden tickets" to the football stadium, parceled out by Democratic operatives to those most committed to the march toward November.

> "WE CALL
> THIS THE NEW
> WEST."
>
> —*former Denver
> city council
> president
> Elbra Wedgeworth,*
> *considered the
> "mother" of the 2008
> Democratic National
> Convention in Denver*

Folks arrived at noon for the 8 PM Obama speech. They came from Europe, from India, from Florida and Alaska and Harlem and suburban Highlands Ranch. They wore sensible shoes, spike heels, combat fatigues, and dashikis. They pulled their kids out of school and fed them hot dogs for eight hours.

Top Democrats still fretted. Would there be enough spectators? Enough toilets? Enough security? Enough enthusiasm? Republicans had successfully hammered Obama's celebrity-over-substance. How arrogant to flaunt the forty-fifth anniversary of the Reverend Martin Luther King Jr.'s landmark "I have a dream" speech. Snarling TV commentators got one look at the Greek columns framing Denver's stage and declared it "Barack-opolis." Wasn't a rock-star stadium appearance the worst possible response?

The doubters didn't ask Pastor Paul Burleson, who spoke of a blessed dream making its way toward Denver. They didn't ask Lakeisha Chestnut of Alabama, who cried tears of joy onstage in Michelle Obama's arms. They didn't ask Herbie Lamarre of New York, who gazed at the stage and said Obama's accepting the Democratic nomination meant that Dr. King had not died in vain. When Wedgeworth felt the rumble of the Invesco Field stands filled with ecstatic, nonfootball customers, she said, "It basically happened the way we always said it would."

In her speech to the Invesco Field crowd, long before the headliners, Wedgeworth restated what had been obscured in a week of hoopla: "We call this the New West." Her words were little noted nor long remembered there, but they were actually the whole point of this 2008 love affair between Denver and the Democrats. Enthusiasts sensed a Democratic presidential candidate could finally win Colorado in November. Rocky Mountain demographics were shifting.

The new battleground states were in the youthful, high-tech, global-economy West. Governors in seven states—Colorado, New Mexico, Kansas, Oklahoma, Montana, Arizona, and Wyoming—had turned from Republican to Democrat since 2002, a remarkable fact underlined by Colorado governor Bill Ritter's hoarse turn in the Invesco Field spotlight. As a Brookings Institution study put it, "The southern Intermountain West is well on its way to earning itself the title of the New American Heartland."

That perfect night in a football stadium, then, was the happy ending to the tale of how the New West and the New American Heartland were won over. Obama strode confidently across a sea of blue carpet to a podium flooded by a wave of camera pops and cell phone flashes.

Obama enjoyed the 84,000 enjoying themselves. But he also submitted a first draft of history for future textbooks. "Tonight, I say to the American people, to Democrats and Republicans and independents across this great land—enough! This moment—this election—is our chance to keep, in the twenty-first century, the American promise alive."

It would be more than two months before Obama could learn whether he was the winner. But as his last words bounced around a stadium of delirious spectators, as fireworks exploded and biodegradable confetti rained down, a city council-woman and a mayor and a governor and a TV audience of 38 million were more than ready to declare a winner: Denver.

For a remarkable week in 2008, Democrats challenged the Rocky Mountain West to rise up and compete in the world of politics. This one was no contest.

MICHAEL BOOTH
The Denver Post
September 12, 2008

"CHANGE HAS SERVED ME WELL. IT HAS SERVED
DENVER WELL OVER ITS 150-YEAR HISTORY."

—*Denver mayor John Hickenlooper*

Leaders of the Denver 2008 Convention Host Committee, above, *started taking their bows Saturday night at the Elitch Gardens media party, spreading out over Denver's seventy-acre amusement park. Key to raising the moxie and the money for Denver's Democratic National Convention bid were, from left, former Denver city council president Elbra Wedgeworth, US Senator Ken Salazar, Lieutenant Governor Barbara O'Brien, Governor Bill Ritter, Denver mayor John Hickenlooper, and Denver lawyer Steve Farber.*

Converting the hoops-and-hockey mecca of the Pepsi Center, opposite page, *into a television-ready political arena consumed millions of dollars and hundreds of workers.*

Art, commerce, and politics mixed easily throughout convention week.
Ron Benson, above, *marketing director for Denver artist Malcolm
Farley, carries an unfinished painting of Barack Obama near Elitch
Gardens before the kickoff media party.*

Some Denver residents and students, right, *get an in-person
preview of the all-important podium at the 2008 Democratic National
Convention just days before the hall would be filled with thousands
of national delegates and journalists from around the world.*

"THIS IS NOT AMERICA. THIS IS WHAT A POLICE STATE LOOKS LIKE."

—Trish Gallagher, a Boston woman protesting in Denver for Code Pink

The $50 million federal grant for Democratic National Convention security included plenty of bright blue handcuffs, evident here as police, above, *take down a protester near the City and County Building on the convention's first day.*

A few protests grew tense, but many more went off smoothly. Aurora police officer Chuck Deshazer, opposite page, *shakes protesters' hands as they march with the Iraq Veterans Against the War from the Denver Coliseum to the Pepsi Center on the third day of the convention.*

Celebrity-spotting was a prime spectator sport throughout the convention, including this 16th Street Mall crowd discovering Angela Bassett outside Hard Rock Café.

Spike Lee was everywhere during convention week, often hiding from admirers while trying to get some work done. Here, the film director joined other celebrities at Hard Rock Café for a Creative Coalition meeting.

One of the largest protests of the week was a Sunday march from Civic Center Park to the Pepsi Center, although crowd totals were closer to 1,000 than the tens of thousands hoped for by march organizers.

"NEITHER REPUBLICANS NOR DEMOCRATS REPRESENT THE PEOPLE."

—Cindy Sheehan, prominent Iraq war protester

A few Denver residents were less than thrilled to be caught up in noisy protests, including *Jennifer Gonzales*, above, *holding her five-year-old daughter, Mielyn. The Unconventional Action protest rolled through downtown Denver on Sunday.*

Some protesters, left, *seek a bigger impact by blocking traffic on Colfax Avenue near Civic Center Park on the Monday of convention week.*

Protest observers were available to provide more objective assessments of police and crowd behavior. Gary Rumor, above left, and Larry Hildes stand in Civic Center Park after police shot tear gas at a crowd during Monday's demonstrations.

Protesters, opposite page, snake past Denver's prime public square, Civic Center Park, on the Sunday march toward the Pepsi Center.

Tiffany Kramer, above, *walks her Democratically dressed dog, Playmate, on the 16th Street Mall before protesters clogged the streets Sunday afternoon.*

Throughout the convention, crowds on the 16th Street Mall, opposite page, *provided some of the economic impact Democratic National Convention organizers were looking for.*

Denver police, above, *use pepper spray on a group of anarchists marching through downtown Denver.*

Amanda Hubbard, left, *pours water in her eyes after getting sprayed with tear gas at Civic Center Park.*

Police forces that some decried as overkill, opposite page, *were poised to swoop down on any protest they deemed was getting out of hand. Supporters and opponents documented their every move on camera.*

Pepper-spray incidents were few, and posed pictures with police were frequent. College students, from left, *Kelsee Rohrer, Natalie Ifland,* and *Britanny Aki* mug for a photo op with a Denver police response team stationed on the 16th Street Mall on Tuesday.

Street entertainment, retail politics, and an endless search for the perfect lunch brought delegates, protesters, and hangers-on to the 16th Street Mall throughout the convention.

Denver hadn't hosted the Democratic convention for 100 years, but the city quickly grew accustomed to floor delegates' love of silly hats and digital self-portraits, above.

Former president Bill Clinton, right, the only Democratic president to be reelected since Franklin Delano Roosevelt, thrills Wednesday's Pepsi Center crowd with a ringing endorsement of Barack Obama, enumerating his qualifications for the White House.

Senator Obama made a "surprise" visit to the Pepsi Center stage on Wednesday, a night before his historic acceptance speech before the throngs at Invesco Field at Mile High. Obama thanked Senator Biden on Wednesday but also pointed up to the Clintons in their box and urged the crowd to honor their work.

Michelle Obama's presence and style had some fans wondering why she wasn't the Obama on the ticket. The candidate's wife, opposite page, claps for the Pepsi Center crowd and later brings down the house with the entrance of her two daughters and a quick video conference with Dad, who was campaigning in the Midwest.

31

"Whether you voted for me or voted for Barack, the time is now to unite as a single party with a single purpose. We are on the same team, and none of us can sit on the sidelines."

—*Senator*
Hillary Rodham Clinton

Senator Hillary Rodham Clinton, far left, *fairly glows onstage during her highly anticipated speech Tuesday, giving a shout-out to her "sisterhood of the traveling pantsuit." Delegates and pundits credited Clinton's speech as a giant step toward party unity.*

Loyal Clinton delegates— joined by younger fans, left—*had threatened a floor fight or other divisive may- hem, but emphatic endorse- ments of the Democratic ticket from their leader brought many to Obama's side.*

33

Delaware senator Joe Biden, above, *was reassuring to some skeptical Obama voters when he was tapped for the vice presidential slot, and at the Pepsi Center he threw a few early campaign punches after a moving introduction by his son.*

Expected to be the smiling assassin during the campaign, Biden was buoyant amid the Denver crowds, left.

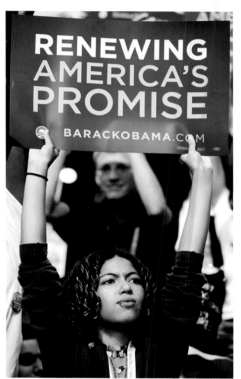

Delegates and unofficial Democrats alternated between wild sign-waving and quietly absorbing the big picture. Above, from left, *Cuba Gooding Sr. flashes a sign as Obama takes the stage at Invesco Field on Thursday; Donna E. King of Chicago listens carefully at Invesco Field; and delegate Jessica Beckett of Poulsbo, Washington, lifts spirits on the floor of the Pepsi Center during Tuesday's speeches.*

Sondra Samuels, opposite page, *a delegate from Minneapolis, claps in agreement as Michelle Obama speaks about her husband at the Pepsi Center. Michelle represented a new kind of role model for some people in the audience.*

"THE WAY [HILLARY RODHAM CLINTON] BROUGHT US TOGETHER,
I HOPE WE CAN ALL MOVE FORWARD. GOD BLESS HER FOR THAT."

—Dunbar Watson Jr., an Obama supporter who had argued with Clinton delegates

Loyal Hillary Rodham Clinton delegates and those just wanting to pay respects to the longtime pol stand on their chairs at the Pepsi Center on Tuesday as she takes the stage for her well-regarded speech.

"FAILURE AT SOME POINT IN EVERYONE'S LIFE IS INEVITABLE,
BUT GIVING UP IS UNFORGIVABLE."

—Democratic vice presidential nominee Senator Joe Biden

Blanca O'Leary and Bryan Gonzales, Colorado delegates from Aspen, catch a glimpse of Senator Joe Biden as he reaches the Pepsi Center floor during the Democratic National Convention on Monday.

"AS A YOUNG PERSON OF COLOR,
IT MEANS THE WORLD TO ME TO
HAVE AN AFRICAN AMERICAN
ACCEPT THIS NOMINATION."

—*Obama fan David Gilbert-Pederson*

*Some delegates were pinned to Obama, including Mississippi's
Kelly Jacobs,* above, *showing off her allegiance on the convention
floor. At right,* Colorado delegate Julia Hicks of Westminster
displays fancy fingernails and a special "Democrats" edition of
Time *magazine.*

After much speculation and anticipation, Massachusetts senator and Kennedy family leader Ted Kennedy rose from his hospital bed to deliver a rousing speech at the Pepsi Center on Monday. Kennedy exhorted Democrats to take back the White House while sticking to traditional party values.

Hillary Rodham and Chelsea Clinton enjoy the floor show from their box while waiting for former president Bill Clinton to speak to the hall on Wednesday.

Michelle Obama and Senator Joe Biden say hello in the Pepsi Center stands during Tuesday's proceedings.

44

Aurora police detective Casey Crowfoot, above, hands out water to people waiting for as long as three hours in the lines at Invesco Field's parking lots.

"WE ADVISED PEOPLE TO COME AS EARLY AS POSSIBLE. THERE IS UNPARALLELED INTEREST IN THIS EVENT."

—*Democratic National Convention spokeswoman Natalie Wyeth*

Crowds for Obama's historic Invesco Field speech were frustrated, but not daunted, by long lines stretching for hours, left.

"I NEVER THOUGHT I WOULD LIVE LONG ENOUGH
TO SEE THIS HAPPEN. I TOLD MY CHILDREN THIS
WOULD NOT HAPPEN IN THEIR LIFETIME, AND
PROBABLY NOT THEIR CHILDREN'S LIFETIME.
MAYBE IN THEIR GRANDCHILDREN'S LIFETIME."

—former Colorado state senator Gloria Tanner

Another newly minted star, Beijing Olympics gold-medal gymnast Shawn Johnson,
above, *shakes hands with members of the Lakewood Police Department SWAT
Team 3 inside Invesco Field at Mile High.*

Tracy Rhines, right, *holds up his nine-month-old son, Eliseo, as the crowd does
the wave at Invesco Field at Mile High.*

46

"HE REALLY, REALLY BELIEVES AMERICANS CAN BE ONE,
CAN LIVE IN PEACE IN THE WORLD COMMUNITY."

—*Oregon state senator Margaret Carter*

Delegates down on the field, above, *spend their time between speeches partying, snacking, and taking endless photos of the enthusiastic crowds.*

Obama's image, opposite page, *was everywhere in Denver: from delegate signs to T-shirt fronts, everybody wanted to display their hero's face.*

"HIS BEING HERE MEANS THAT MARTIN LUTHER KING [JR.] DID NOT DIE IN VAIN."

—Herbie Lamarre,
an Obama supporter inside Invesco Field

The official nomination of the first African American candidate in major-party history was enough to move many spectators to tears, including Lakeisha Chestnut, above, who came from Birmingham, Alabama, for Obama's groundbreaking speech.

His big moment finally here, Senator Barack Obama, left, strides out across a sea of blue carpet and greets a wild crowd of 84,000 for the first outdoor presidential-nomination acceptance speech since John F. Kennedy's.

"AMERICA, NOW IS NOT THE TIME FOR SMALL PLANS."

—Senator Barack Obama, accepting his party's nomination at Invesco Field

The big day was long for everybody, particularly the candidates' families. Sasha Obama, above, *leans for the comfort of her mother's lap as Michelle Obama, Jill and Joe Biden, and the Bidens' daughter, Ashley, watch Obama speak at Invesco Field.*

Senator Barack Obama, opposite page, *claps for the 84,000 who made their way into Invesco Field in search of the promise of change.*

Those who couldn't score a "golden ticket" for the stadium found other ways to get involved in history. Top, from left, *Melanie Schultz, Dan Reeves, Carmen Denker, and Kevin Rhoades gather on a front lawn on Twenty-first Street in Jefferson Park to watch Barack Obama's speech on television.*

A woman, above, *looks out a window at Angel's Sports Bar toward the twilight gathering of Invesco Field's crowds.*

From the nosebleed seats in the stadium, right, *Obama's speech is a mosaic of flags, signs calling for change, and the cell phone camera flashes of the amassed political faithful.*

"AMERICA, WE CANNOT TURN BACK. WE CANNOT WALK ALONE. AT THIS MOMENT, IN THIS ELECTION, WE MUST PLEDGE ONCE MORE TO MARCH INTO THE FUTURE."

—*Senator Barack Obama, in his acceptance speech*

Critics attacked the Invesco Field stage as "Barack-opolis," the Greek temple of Obama; others considered it a replica of the White House.

Obama's biggest moment lasted for about forty-two minutes of speech-making; more than 38 million people watched on television.

M. A. De Muirier, above, *of Lakewood, salutes Obama's speech on the last day of the Democratic National Convention.*

Lakeisha Chestnut and Holley Camp, both from Alabama, hold hands, left, *while listening to Obama's speech.*

The Obama and Biden families, opposite page, *share congratulatory hugs in the wake of the big speech.*

"YOUR INSIDES JUST RAISE UP. IT'S LIKE A FIRE
INSIDE YOU. IT WAS OVERWHELMING."

—*Invesco Field spectator Sharon Fargalla*

A multigenerational mix of the Obama and Biden families, above, *celebrate onstage as the Democrats prepare to say good-bye and hit the campaign trail through the November election.*

With the applause swelling in the aftermath of his speech, Obama brings back his family for a final bow, opposite page. *Sasha holds his hand, while older sister Malia walks out with Michelle Obama.*

Contemplative or just plain tired, Dave Turk, above, of Washington, DC, collects his thoughts and his energy following Obama's speech.

"PART OF THE BENEFIT IS NOT HOW THE WORLD
LOOKS AT US, BUT HOW WE LOOK AT OURSELVES.
PART OF BEING A GREAT CITY IS BELIEVING
IN YOURSELF. TAKING ON A CHALLENGE AND
PULLING IT OFF COMPLETES THAT BELIEF."

—Denver mayor John Hickenlooper

Stagehand Tom Dunman, left, of Memphis, Tennessee, carries the podium flags away after the convention's rousing finish.

Book photo editing by Meghan Lyden and Tim Rasmussen

Introduction and captions by *The Denver Post* staff writer Michael Booth

Photographic imaging by Don Pavlin

Book layout and design by Margaret McCullough

DEMOCRATIC NATIONAL CONVENTION COVERAGE TEAM

The Denver Post photographers
Lyn Alweis
Joe Amon
Brian Brainerd
Hyoung Chang
Andy Cross
Karl Gehring
John Leyba
Cyrus McCrimmon
Steve Nehf
John Prieto
Noah Rabinowitz
RJ Sangosti
Kathryn Scott Osler
Craig F. Walker

Photo editors
Mateo Leyba
Eric Lutzens
Meghan Lyden
Ken Lyons
Reza Marvashti
Tim Rasmussen
John Sunderland

Online photo editors
Mathew Luschek
Galen Nathanson
Deb Neeley
Don Pavlin
Chelsy Shore

MEDIANEWS GROUP
Photographers
Michael Baker
Craig Cunningham
Rick Egan
Jeff Gritchen
Jason Halley
Sean Hiller
Julia Malakie
Lindsay Pierce
David Royal

Photo editor
Bob Houlihan

FREELANCE
Photographers
Nathan Armes
Dana Romanoff
Evan Semon

Photo editors
Glenn Asakawa
Alison Dale

This publication is provided for informational and educational purposes. The information herein contained is true and complete to the best of our knowledge.

ISBN-13: 978-1-55591-720-3

Printed in Canada by Friesens Corp.

10 9 8 7 6 5 4 3 2

Fulcrum Publishing
4690 Table Mountain Dr., Ste. 100
Golden, CO 80403
800-992-2908
303-277-1623
www.fulcrumbooks.com